FRIDA KAHLO

Mysterious Painter

by
Nancy Frazier

A BLACKBIRCH PRESS BOOK

WOODBRIDGE, CONNECTICUT

Published by Blackbirch Press, Inc.
260 Amity Road
Woodbridge, CT 06525

©1992 Blackbirch Press, Inc.
First Edition

Printed in China

10 9 8 7 6 5 4

Library of Congress Cataloging-in-Publication Data

Frazier, Nancy
    Frida Kahlo: mysterious painter/by Nancy Frazier.
      p.   cm. — (The Library of famous women)
    Includes bibliographical references and index.
    Summary: Examines the life of the twentieth-century Mexican painter
known for her self-portraits and the loneliness and pain that were reflected in
her work.
    ISBN 1-56711-012-6
    1. Kahlo, Frida—Juvenile literature. 2. Painters—Mexico—Biogra-
phy—Juvenile literature. [1. Kahlo, Frida. 2. Women artists. 3. Artists]
I. Title. II. Series.
ND259.K33F68   1992
759.972—dc20
[B]   92-25810
                                                   CIP
                                                     AC

Contents

Chapter 1

Strange Beauty

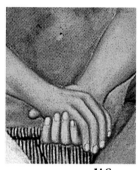

Frida Kahlo was among Mexico's most outstanding artists. Some people believe that she was the country's greatest.

A detail from *The Two Fridas.*

Frida died at age 47, after living far less than an average life span. She left behind more than 200 works. Most were paintings of herself. In almost all of her self-portraits she is both beautiful and strange. In her self-portraits, as in all her paintings, she challenges us to understand her life, her time, and what she believed.

The Two Fridas is one of Frida Kahlo's most powerful but puzzling works. In this double self-portrait, the same person is seen in two different ways. The Frida on the left wears a beautiful, lacy, white gown. It looks like a Victorian wedding dress. The Frida on the right wears a peasant skirt and a blouse that show the shape of her body. The skirt is the color of earth; the blouse is the color of sky and it is trimmed with gold, the color of the sun.

(Opposite page)
The Two Fridas, **painted in 1939, was inspired by Frida's childhood desire to have a friend just like her.**

Strangest of all, in *The Two Fridas*, the artist has painted her heart—*two* hearts, actually—*outside* her two bodies. One heart is whole, the other has been cut or broken open. The hearts are connected by an artery (vein) that starts in a small picture the darker Frida holds in her hand. It is a picture of her husband, Diego Rivera, when he was a boy. The artery winds around from one Frida to the other. It comes to an end, clamped by a surgeon's scissors, dripping blood onto the skirt of the Frida dressed in white.

Frida finished *The Two Fridas* while she and Rivera were being divorced. The darker Frida who holds his picture, and whose heart is whole, is the woman whom Rivera loved. The elegant, cool, married woman in white is the one whose heart he broke.

If you cover everything but the heads, the faces are *almost* identical but not quite. The complexion of the woman in white seems a bit lighter, perhaps fresher. Is she prettier? Or is it just that the elegant white dress and the light clouds around her head soften her face?

The faces of *The Two Fridas* show no emotion. In fact, the artist never reveals her feelings in her painting through smiles or

frowns. And she is never doing anything—
never running, dancing, fighting, painting,
cooking, or playing. Still, the impact of
her mood is strong. It is revealed by the
background of the work, an angry swirl of
dark clouds that suggests dangerous, stormy
weather.

The two Fridas gaze forward, but they are
not really looking *at* anything. The eyes of
the figures almost seem glazed over. The
faces show no emotion; not anger, nor fear,
nor pleasure.

The World of the Surreal

Nothing is ordinary or real in *The Two
Fridas.* The scene has the bizarre atmosphere
of a dream—perhaps a nightmare. It was
painted in 1939. During that time a
strange style called *surrealism* was popular
among European artists.

Surrealists freed themselves from showing people and things as they appear in the
everyday world. They believed there was "a
more-real-than-real world behind the real."
This was the "super-real" world of dreams
and imagination. Sometimes it was called
the world of the *subconscious* mind. That is
the part of our minds that thinks without
our realizing it. A painting by Salvador
Dali called *The Persistence of Memory* is one

of the best examples of surrealism. In it Dali shows limp watches draped over strange objects.

The genius of Frida Kahlo, like many of the European surrealists, is that she tells so much with so few details. Yet everything in her painting is *symbolic* of something else. Even things that are missing are symbolic.

Without trees and plants and furniture, the landscape of *The Two Fridas* is empty. That makes clear that the two Fridas are very much alone. The hand each Frida holds for comfort is her own hand.

When Frida was six years old she became very ill. During this time she was isolated. She invented a make-believe world. She entered that world by fogging a window pane with her warm breath. She drew a door on the window fog, and her imagination took her through the door. In the fantasy world she created, she had a friend, a happy child, who danced and laughed. The make-believe friend listened to little Frida's problems and cheered her up.

When the adult Frida discussed painting *The Two Fridas*, she remembered her imaginary playmate. She wrote, "Thirty-four years have passed since I experienced this magic friendship and every time that I remember it, it revives and becomes larger

❖

In 1939, many European artists were doing paintings that showed the "super-real" world of dreams and imagination.

and larger inside of my world." The painting shows the truth: Frida is lonely and she
is her own best friend.

This double portrait also hints at Frida's
two-fold heritage—the elegant, fragile
European lady dressed in white, and the
sturdy Mexican-Indian woman in a peasant
dress. Frida inherited both worlds from
her parents. But it was her Mexican roots
that gained her devotion and attention.

The Spirit of Mexico

With one giant step you can cross from
the United States into Mexico. When you
do, you enter a different world. It is a
world as colorful as the brilliant flower
called a "bird of paradise" that grows there.
Real birds just as beautiful live there. Palm
trees and geraniums grow wild. Mexican
clothes are richly embroidered in dark
purples, crimsons, and reds.

The music of Mexico is full of spirit and
the sound of guitars, violins, and brass
trumpets. Music plays a major part even in
religious holidays, which are celebrated
with *fiestas*. These festivals feature parades,
fireworks, floats, and lively dances that last
until dawn.

Mexico is a gorgeous and exciting country. Frida was deeply attached to the land

Ancient sculptures remain at the Chichén Itzá site in Mexico. Frida's art was greatly influenced by ancient Mexican artwork.

and its history. Even her most personal portraits relate to the people and customs of her homeland.

The Frida on the right in *The Two Fridas* is dressed in the sort of skirt and blouse that might have been worn by native women of a tribe called "Tehuanas." According to their legends, Tehuanas came to Mexico many centuries ago, from a country where the sun never set and it never rained. A great river ran through their land and the soil was said to be blessed with fertility— except that some years there was terrible drought. It was during such a dry spell that the Tehuanas rowed off in boats toward the sunset, stopping along the way to find a favorable place to settle.

The stories say that the men rowed and rowed and became very thin. The women, with nothing to do, became healthy and stronger than the men. The women took charge. A princess became the head of the expedition. They had many adventures and eventually settled on the Isthmus of Tehuantepec in southern Mexico. The women have long been known for strength, intelligence, and beauty. They are also in control of the business and finance. They dominate Tehuana men.

Although she loved their folklore and costumes, Frida was not a true Tehuana woman. When she and her husband had problems, she was the one who suffered more. But her marriage was only part of the subject of her art, just as it was only a part of her life.

When she was asked why she painted so many self-portraits, Frida answered, "Because I am alone."

She married a famous artist. She, herself, became recognized as an artist. Her friends were some of the richest and most exciting people in the world. Her life should have glittered with delight and happiness. There were pleasures. But she also suffered great sadness and enormous pain. When she said she was alone, she meant that she was lonely. Happiness is easily shared. Sadness and pain are not.

Family Tree

The pleasant community of Coyoacán is about an hour away from the loud and crowded capital of Mexico City. On a street corner in Coyoacán is the house where Frida Kahlo was born on July 6, 1907.

If you blend the blue of a summer sky with the purple of an iris—that is the color of the Kahlo house. It is like many Mexican houses in style, with thick stucco walls facing the street and an open courtyard inside. From the street the house is plain, but enter the courtyard and you are in a wonderful, secret world. It is filled with trees and flowers that bloom year-round.

The brilliant blue Kahlo house is the shape of a *U*. The center of the *U* is a patio with lush plants and flowers. Water sprays from fountains, and a small concrete pyramid is covered with an old Mexican sculpture.

(Opposite page)
Frida's famous blue house in Mexico City.

13

Two giant "Judas figures" guard the entrance to the Kahlo house.

Rooms of the house open onto the patio. These rooms are still much as they were when Frida lived there toward the end of her life. An unfinished painting sits on the easel. Paintbrushes on a table look as if she had put them down only minutes ago to run an errand in town.

The house is filled with Frida's furniture and the things she collected. Many of her own paintings hang on the walls. Even her clothes, her jewelry, her letters and books, and her dolls are there.

At the entrance to the blue house are two enormous *papier mâché* men, called "Judas figures." Figures like these were burned or blown up, like firecrackers, during the Friday before Easter. Frida loved these figures and usually had them around the house. They also appear in her paintings.

Frida Kahlo's house is now a museum. Thousands of people visit the location every year. Though she is gone, Frida's spirit is at home there.

Frida's Childhood Home

When Frida lived in Coyoacán as a child, her house was painted white. It was different inside, too. Instead of her Mexican-style furniture and personal mementos, her parents had heavy furniture, dark oriental rugs, lacy curtains, and somber drapes. That is how well-to-do Mexicans decorated their homes at the time. The style was European rather than native Mexican.

In a painting called *My Grandparents, My Parents, and I,* Frida painted her house. She stands in the center of the courtyard, a little girl holding a ribbon. Behind her are her mother, Matilde, and father, Guillermo. They appear almost exactly as they looked in their wedding photograph. But, just as she painted her heart outside her body in *The Two Fridas,* here Frida painted herself, still unborn, outside her mother's body. Behind Frida's parents are their parents.

Pre-Columbian sculptures fill the backyard garden at the Kahlo house.

Frida's mother, Matilde Calderón, was beautiful. Matilde's maternal grandfather was a Spanish general and her maternal grandmother had Indian blood. Matilde Calderón de Kahlo was a devout Catholic who took her four daughters to church every Sunday and made them pray before their meals. She kept her house spotless and taught her children the arts of house-keeping, sewing, and embroidery. She was stern and strict.

In the painting of her family, the artist placed herself in front of her father. Frida's small head is about where her father's heart would be. That is not by chance. Frida was his favorite child.

When he was born in Germany, her father's name was Wilhelm Kahlo. His parents were Jewish. Wilhelm's father was a jeweler and sold photographic supplies. Photography was a new invention then.

Wilhelm was a university student when he had a serious accident. After that, he began to suffer from epilepsy. Once called "falling sickness," epilepsy causes its victims to suddenly lose control of their senses and bodies. They collapse and often become unconscious. Usually, when they wake, they don't remember what happened.

At about the same time, Wilhelm's mother died and his father remarried. His epileptic attacks caused Wilhelm to leave the university. As he did not like his new stepmother, he decided to leave Germany entirely. His father gave him money to travel by ship to Mexico. So it was then that, at the age of 19, Wilhelm left his homeland and never returned. He changed his name to Guillermo Kahlo.

Guillermo Kahlo married a Mexican woman. When their second child was born, his wife died. Then he married Frida's mother, Matilde. Both Matilde and Guillermo were working in a jewelry shop

❖

Frida was her father's favorite child.

in Mexico City. For a reason that has never been explained, the Kahlos did not bring Guillermo's oldest daughters to live in the new household. They were sent away to a convent and visited only occasionally.

Guillermo took up photography. He became skilled and well known in the profession. Painting was a hobby he enjoyed. The Kahlos had two children and built their house in Coyoacán before Frida was born. They had one more daughter after Frida, and then their family of four was complete.

A Special Relationship

Frida admired her father. It was when she first became seriously ill that she and he became especially close.

Frida remembers that her sickness began with a terrible pain in her leg. The disease was polio. Like epilepsy, polio affects the nervous system. Because it affected so many children, it was also called "infantile paralysis." Instead of causing seizures (attacks) and unconsciousness, polio often left people crippled.

Frida's nine-month-long recovery from polio kept her at home. It left her with one leg very weak and thinner than the other. The doctor told her parents that exercise would help her leg grow strong. Her father made sure that she played in such sports as soccer, boxing, wrestling, and swimming. She liked to climb trees and play ball—both very unusual for a girl in those years.

Her thin leg did grow stronger, but it never grew to match the other in size. Frida was self-conscious about that, and always looked for ways to hide it. Other children teased her, and she felt left out. It was probably the first time a feeling of loneliness overcame her.

Guillermo Kahlo, himself ill for so long, was sensitive to Frida's suffering. He saw much of himself in her and sometimes said, "Frida is the most intelligent of my daughters. She is the most like me."

Frida's father often shared books and his interest in nature with her. They went together to the parks around their home. She collected plants and insects and studied them. Sometimes she watched while he enjoyed his hobby of painting with watercolors. Sometimes she was taken on his photography trips. He was hired by the government to take pictures of the important buildings of the country.

Her father taught Frida about the ancient world of Mexico. He showed her how to

❖

As a child, Frida suffered from polio, which affects the nervous system and often cripples its victims.

use a camera and to develop photographs. He also taught her how to touch up the photographs and to color them by hand.

Though they were close to each other, neither Matilde nor Guillermo Kahlo showed much affection to their children. Strangely, the two oldest daughters from Guillermo's first marriage were not welcomed into the home. Matilde's first child, who was also named Matilde, ran away from home at age 15 to be with the man she loved. The girl tried many times to make peace with her parents. She brought gifts of fruit and left them outside the door, since her mother would not let her come in. For 12 years, the older Matilde, Señora Matilde Kahlo, remained stern and unforgiving. Finally, she made peace with her daughter.

Although he warmed to Frida, Guillermo Kahlo kept a cool distance from the rest of his family. When he came home from work, he usually went into a room to play the piano and closed the door behind him. Then he ate supper alone and in silence.

Despite her suffering in those early years, and the stern discipline of her home, Frida Kahlo loved her parents dearly. She also developed a healthy appetite for fun—she was often full of mischief.

Chapter 3

The Rebels

According to her birth certificate, Frida Kahlo was born in 1907. But according to Frida herself, she was born in 1910. She was not pretending to be younger than her real age. Rather, she wanted to say that her life began in a year of overwhelming importance to her country. That year, 1910, was when the Mexican Revolution began.

The first goal of the revolutionaries was to overthrow the government of General Porfirio Díaz. The General had been in charge some 34 years. He had brought new wealth to Mexico, but only for a few people. A good deal of this prosperity was in the hands of foreign investors. Most of the population was very poor. These were the people who rose up to overthrow Díaz.

Díaz was defeated and forced to leave Mexico. But the governments that followed him could not bring peace. The

One of Frida's earliest self-portraits, painted in the late 1920s.

(Opposite page) Emiliano Zapata was a farmer who became a hero in the Mexican Revolution.

fighting continued and lasted for 10 years. One popular hero of the revolution was Pancho Villa. He was an ex-bandit who organized cowboys of northern Mexico into an army. In the south, another hero was a farmer named Emiliano Zapata who led a group of poor peasants in their fight.

The spirit and energy of the revolution brought hope to the masses for whom life was so hard. The idea of the revolution was also important to middle-class, more educated Mexicans like Frida Kahlo who believed in equality. Although Frida was only three years old when the revolution began, she grew up in an atmosphere inspired by its beliefs.

Studies in Mexico City

In 1922, when she was 15, Frida went to the finest high school in the country, the National Preparatory School in Mexico City. It was a part of the University of Mexico. Her mother did not favor the idea. It was her father who encouraged that part of Frida's education. She rode the trolley—an electric train that ran on tracks along the street—an hour to school, and then another hour back home again.

Although 2,000 students attended the school, only 35 were girls. Besides the

Pancho Villa (center) organized cowboys into an army in northern Mexico and became a hero of the Mexican Revolution.

inequality between rich and poor, there was also an obvious inequality between males and females. But Frida was already an exceptional young woman. She was planning to become a physician.

During her first days at school, she dressed as a proper European schoolgirl. Besides her dark-blue skirt, white blouse, and stockings, she wore a black straw hat with a ribbon.

Frida made many new friends in school. She also became a member of a group that called itself the Cachuchas. The name came from the boat-shaped hats that the members wore. The seven boys and two girls in this group were known for their mischief as well as their intelligence. Some of their pranks were cruel—winding firecrackers around a dog and lighting them, for example. Some pranks were dangerous, such as setting off a firecracker in the window of a crowded classroom. And, in one instance, they rode a donkey through the school corridors.

But the Cachuchas also had admirable qualities. They competed to see who could find the best books to read or who could finish a book first. They filled their imaginations with adventures from the stories they read, and they made up their own

In school, Frida became a member of a group of friends that called themselves the Cachuchas, named for the hats they wore.

adventures to tell one another. Most of all, they were boldly independent.

The Cachuchas were also passionate about the ideals of a new Mexico. They wanted a Mexico that was less influenced by foreigners than it had been before the revolution. While Díaz had been the president, the upper classes had imitated French and Spanish culture. Díaz himself had powdered his dark skin to hide the Indian blood in his veins. The Cachuchas, on the other hand, believed in the native honor and heritage of the Mexican people themselves.

A few months after she started school, Frida stopped wearing her blue skirt and white blouse. She cut her long black hair and went to school in overalls. She was showing that she was no longer following European tradition. She also wanted to show that she was on the side of ordinary working people rather than the wealthy class.

"Turn your eyes to the soil of Mexico, to our customs and our traditions, our hopes and our wishes, to what we in truth are!" advised a philosopher and teacher at the National Preparatory School. Frida and her friends took these ideas to heart. They proudly became part of a movement to return Mexico to Mexicans.

❖

The Cachuchas were passionate about the ideals of Mexico and wanted their country to be less influenced by foreigners.

Mexico's Rich Heritage

The land now called Mexico had several brilliant native civilizations before the Spanish landed there in the 16th century. The earliest *Mesoamerican* culture we know of was made up of people who lived in villages along the Gulf of Mexico more than 3,000 years ago. They were called *Olmecs*. Some people believe the Olmecs were the mother culture of all civilizations of Mexico.

The Olmecs lived in settlements of hundreds and sometimes thousands of people. They built huge stone pyramids. But most astonishing was their art. They carved huge heads out of stone that we marvel at to this day. They may even have developed a form of writing. Archaeologists have discovered evidence of the existence of a complex Olmec culture, but can only guess what Olmec life was really like. It is also unknown just why Olmec civilization came to an end about 2,000 years ago.

Other civilizations followed the Olmecs. It was the Mayans who hacked away at the jungle to build spectacular temples and palaces. They also produced excellent paintings and sculpture. The Mayans invented a system of mathematics and an alphabet. They used two calendars. One

The Art of the Mayans

The Mayans built a magnificent civilizaton in the jungles of Mexico about 2,000 years ago. In addition to great feats of engineering and architecture, the Mayans fostered a rich artistic culture.

At top right is a carved stone vase made almost 1500 years ago. Below is a *fresco* painting (done directly on a wall) that depicts a Mayan battle scene.

At left is an Aztec sculpture of Xochipilli, god of flowers. Below is a stone sculpture of Quetzalcóatl, Aztec god of life and death.

The Art of the Aztecs

The Aztec civilization, established in Mexico City nearly 700 years ago, was similar to Mayan culture in its devotion to arts and crafts. The Aztecs felt a close bond with nature and developed many rituals for worshiping the sun and other natural forces. About 650 years later, Frida Kahlo would use Aztec beliefs as inspiration for her work.

A giant Mayan temple stands at Chichén Itzá, near Mexico City.

was like ours, with 365 days in a year. The other calendar was shorter, but every day had its own signs and meaning. The Mayans believed the day on which you were born might determine the day on which you were married. According to their calendar, on some days planting was not allowed. The Mayan civilization ended about 1,000 years ago.

The powerful Aztecs who followed the Mayans worshiped a god-king. They believed that humans had to be sacrificed in order to be sure the sun would rise every day. Thousands of people were killed in Aztec rituals. The dead were often eaten by the living. However, Aztecs also loved flowers, enjoyed poetry, and appreciated the beauty of nature. They believed that the dead spent their time in paradise.

The Arrival of Cortez

In 1519, the Spanish conqueror Hernán Cortez arrived in Mexico. He landed with 11 ships, 600 men, 16 horses, and many guns and cannons. He found that the Aztecs who were in power had built a complex system of cities, towns, villages, and roads. The Aztecs had developed their own agriculture and sold their goods and produce in markets. And they also had built great pyramids and other majestic places of worship.

Cortez and his troops marched from the coast into the Aztec capital, which was near Mexico City. The Aztec king, Montezuma, welcomed the Spanish soldiers. Cortez fooled Montezuma and his people into believing that he, Cortez, was the ancestral god Quetzalcóatl.

The king and many of his people were killed by the Spaniards, who went on to take over all of Mexico. The Spanish ruled Mexico for 300 years.

The time before the Spanish came to the New World—before Christopher Columbus landed—is called "pre-Columbian." Art

Spanish conqueror Hernán Cortez arrived in Mexico City in 1519.

and architecture made before the Spanish arrived is also called pre-Columbian. This was the tradition and art that Frida Kahlo learned to cherish. Artists of her day often looked back at pre-Columbian Mexico for inspiration.

The First Sight of Diego

Because they believed in public art, rather than paintings made to hang in rich people's houses, the important artists of Mexico's revolution began to paint pictures on walls—*murals* that everyone could see. Mexico's first important public mural was created by the country's most famous painter of the time, Diego Rivera. The wall he painted was in the auditorium of the National Preparatory School, where Frida was a student.

The size of the wall to be painted was enormous. It was the back wall of the stage. The subject of the mural was a scene from the Creation in the Bible. A man rising out of the Tree of Life symbolized the Creative Force. Two naked figures were symbolic of Man and Woman. The other figures were female and represented such subjects as Knowledge, Tragedy, Poetry, Tradition, Strength, Hope, Charity, and Wisdom. All the figures were much larger than life, and all were painted in rich, bright colors. The mix of light- and dark-skinned figures showed the mix of races that had peopled Mexico.

It took Diego Rivera a year to complete the school's mural. It was not a pretty or a glamorous picture. Many people found it ugly. It certainly created a lot of questions about the meaning and purpose of art.

Rivera was a rather fat and odd-looking man. He liked to wear a huge cowboy hat and work boots. He had to stand on scaffolding for many hours to complete the mural. The students talked about him and about his reputation for chasing women.

Students were not allowed to be in the auditorium while Rivera was at work. But Frida managed to hide and watch him several times. Sometimes she called out to tease him about his pretty models. She took food out of his lunch basket. She even played a mean trick of soaping the stairs down from the stage where he was painting.

It was several years later that Frida and Diego Rivera actually met and fell in love. Before that time, Frida loved one of the Cachuchas, Alejandro Gómez Arias.

Students were not allowed in the auditorium where Rivera was at work, but Frida managed to hide and watch him several times.

Chapter 4

Love and Tragedy

Alejandro Gómez Arias was the leader of the Cachuchas. Older than Frida, he was a young man who was intelligent, athletic, and amusing. He held himself and his friends to the highest standards, and he was well respected. He practiced the art of public speaking with great drama, telling listeners to give themselves to the great future of their country.

During the summer of 1923, Frida and Alejandro fell in love. After school, they spent as much time as they could together. When they were apart, they wrote letters to each other. Frida often decorated her letters with funny drawings.

Young women were not free to meet and date young men in those days, especially in Mexico. It was difficult to enjoy romance. Frida had to invent many excuses for leaving home, not only to see Alejandro in secret, but also to send letters to him. He had to sign his letters to her with the name of a girl.

"Alex," Frida wrote on December 16, 1923, "I am very sorry that yesterday my mother would not let me go to Mexico [City] because they told her there was a *bola* [her word for the fighting that still broke out occasionally] . . . .

"Tomorrow, Monday, I am going to tell her that I have an exam . . . and I will spend the whole day in Mexico, it's not very certain since first I have to see what humor my *mamicíta* ["little mother," an affectionate term] is in and after that decide to tell this lie. . . ."

For two years, Frida and Alejandro saw each other as often as possible. They made plans to visit the United States. "It is good that we should do something in life don't you think so, since we'll be nothing but dopes if we spend our whole life in Mexico . . ." she wrote him.

Frida would have liked to have saved money for a trip to the United States, but her family had fallen on difficult times and she had to help out. She worked during vacations and after school to contribute to the Kahlo household. She was a cashier for a time, then a factory worker, and even a printer's helper.

During the summer of 1923, Frida and Alejandro Gómez Arias fell in love.

A Terrible Accident

Late in the afternoon of September 17, 1925, Frida and Alejandro were aboard a crowded bus going to Coyoacán. They were sitting together in the back of the bus when a trolley with two cars approached. The trolley traveled slowly along its tracks. Like an accident in a dream that cannot be stopped, the collision of the trolley and the bus seemed destined to happen.

The trolley just kept coming, squeezing the bus until the sides of the bus gave out. Then the bus seemed to break into thousands of pieces as the trolley kept running on its tracks. The trolley crushed people who fell beneath it as well as those who were inside the bus.

The seriousness of Frida's injury was almost unimaginable. "A handrail pierced me the way a sword pierces a bull," she once wrote. But it was much worse. The railing went through her body. She was like shattered crystal. Her spine was broken in three places. Her collarbone and her ribs were broken. Her right leg was broken in 11 places. Her foot was twisted and crushed. Her shoulder was twisted out of place. Her pelvis was broken in three places.

Somehow the force of the impact had ripped off all her clothes. A packet of gold colored dust that someone had been carrying sprayed into the air, covering Frida all over. Her blood streaked through the gold.

Lying there in the bus, Frida looked like a surrealist painting. Terrible. Strange. Beyond understanding. People who saw her and did not understand what had happened thought Frida was a performer. Perhaps a dancer. *"La bailarina, la bailarina!"* they cried in Spanish.

The ambulance took Frida to a Red Cross Hospital. Nobody thought she would be able to survive. For a month she lay in a hospital bed. She was enclosed in a plaster cast that was surrounded by a wooden box —almost as if she were buried alive.

The tragedy stunned her parents. Both of them became so ill, they were not able to visit Frida in the hospital for most of the time she was there. But her sister Matilde went every day, and her visits were a great comfort to Frida. Matilde told jokes and cheered up everyone in the ward.

Alejandro was also hurt in the accident, though not as badly as Frida. He had to stay home to recover, but other Cachuchas came to see Frida. She wrote Alejandro many letters. In one she said, "In this hospital, death dances around my bed at night."

"A handrail pierced me the way a sword pierces a bull," Frida once wrote of the accident.

Recovery and Discovery

On October 17, exactly a month after the bus accident, Frida went home from the hospital. Over the next few months, she and Alejandro quarrelled. He learned that she had been unfaithful to him. In letters, she pleaded with him to forgive her.

At first Frida seemed to be recovering well. Then, a year after the accident, it was found that her spine and foot were not set properly. That meant more surgery. For the rest of her life, Frida would suffer the pain of her injuries and of more than 30 operations.

The First Paintings

Forced to sit still, Frida began to paint. Her mother had a special holder made to serve as an easel so that Frida could paint while in bed. Frida began by painting her friends. During the summer of 1926, she started her first important self-portrait.

The artists' unique talent was first seen in this painting. It also showed that she knew the history of art, for she had studied many of the world's greatest artists. Besides the influence of works that she admired from centuries past, her self-portrait showed a more modern style. It is interesting, however, that in this painting there is no trace of the influence of famous Mexican artists of her day, like Diego Rivera.

Frida's self-portrait was a special gift for Alejandro. She wished it to have the magic effect of bringing him back to her. That was not to be. During the next year, while Frida was at home recovering from her operations and painting with more serious purpose, Alejandro was off traveling in Europe. Even when he returned home, their love was never as it had been before the accident.

Frida's self-portrait was a special gift for Alejandro. She wished it to have the magic effect of bringing him back to her.

Chapter 5

The Great Rivera

Diego Rivera in 1932.

Colorful legends are always woven around the lives of famous people. How Frida teased Diego Rivera while he was painting the Creation mural is one such story. Another legend surrounds their meeting five years later, in 1928.

By that time, Frida had a new group of friends in Mexico City. Her closest friend was an Italian-born photographer, Tina Modotti. Tina was the lover of an exiled Cuban Communist. He was assassinated by a gunman while Tina was walking with him on the street. Another young man, whom Frida was very fond of, was also killed.

The political atmosphere of Mexico in 1928 was still dangerous. Frida's new circle of friends believed in communism, and she, too, joined the Communist party. Rivera was also a member. They had probably met at one of the weekly gatherings held at Tina Modotti's house. But that was before their famous encounter that has since become part of legend. Their meeting took place at the Mexican Ministry of Public Education where Rivera painted his second mural between 1923 and 1928.

Once again, Rivera was working while standing on scaffolding. Frida called up to him. This time it was not to tease. As soon as she was well enough to travel, Frida took some paintings to the Ministry to show him. "Diego, come down," she said. When he did, she boldly told him, "Look, I have not come to flirt or anything even if you are a woman-chaser. I have come to show you my painting. If you are interested in it, tell me so; if not, likewise, so that I will go to work at something else to help my parents."

A detail from *Creation* by Diego Rivera. It was while Rivera was painting this mural that he first saw Frida.

Diego Remembers

In his autobiography, Diego's account of their meeting is more detailed and colorful. The day she came to see him was one of the happiest days of his life, he wrote. He describes how beautiful she appeared. He especially admired her dark hair and eyebrows that, he said, "seemed like the wings of a blackbird, their black arches framing two extraordinary brown eyes."

Diego recalled her saying how important it was for her to earn money. He answered,

"In my opinion, no matter how difficult it is for you, you must continue to paint."

Frida told Diego her name and gave him her address so that he would come and see more of her work. They began to spend a great deal of time with each other. He painted her as a figure in one of his murals at the Ministry. Wearing a red work shirt with a red star symbolizing communism, she is handing out weapons to fighters for the cause in which they both believed.

At the Ministry, Rivera's subject matter changed. Instead of standing for virtues like poetry and music, as at the school, now his figures symbolized the Mexican working classes and their struggle for freedom. He concentrated on the Indians of Mexico. He loved their physical features, costumes, and handcrafts. He treasured and collected pre-Columbian art.

Encouraged by Diego, Frida painted with new energy and self-confidence. She also became more interested in Mexican themes, native art, and folklore. For a short time her work resembled Diego Rivera's, but soon she developed her own individual style. He painted huge murals to explain ideas. She showed the world through a few subjects: objects, animals, and people—especially herself.

❖

Encouraged by Diego, Frida painted with new energy and self-confidence. She also became more interested in Mexican themes, native art, and folklore.

It was not long before Frida began to talk of marriage. Frida's mother did not want her to marry a man who was so much older than Frida. Besides, he had been divorced, was a Communist, and had a reputation for chasing women.

Frida's father was less opposed to the marriage. The family could not afford to pay Frida's continuing medical expenses. It even seemed they might have to give up their house. Guillermo Kahlo knew that Diego would be able to take care of his daughter. Diego did more than that. Soon after the marriage took place, he paid off the mortgage on the Kahlos' Coyoacán house.

Frida and Diego in Mexico City, about 1939.

Frida and Diego Are Married

The wedding took place in the city hall at Coyoacán with the mayor officiating. Three local people were there as witnesses. Frida's father attended the wedding, but her mother did not. According to the newspaper report, "The marriage service was unpretentious; it was celebrated in a very cordial atmosphere and with all modesty, without ostentation, and without pompous ceremonies. The *novios* [newlyweds] were warmly congratulated after the marriage by a few intimate friends."

Frida and Diego moved to a fine house in a wealthy section of Mexico City. Although Rivera was an official in the Communist party, the leaders of the party became unhappy with him. They believed he was too friendly with rich business people. Rivera was forced to leave the party, but there was a strange twist to his being expelled. He himself had to announce the charges against him, saying, "I, Diego Rivera, general secretary of the Mexican Communist party, accuse the painter Diego Rivera of collaborating with the petit-bourgeois [rich] government of Mexico and of having accepted a commission to paint the stairway of the national Palace of Mexico. This contradicts the politics of the Comintern. . . . "

Despite his official break with the party, Rivera remained a Communist at heart. His paintings continued to show his deep devotion to the party's ideals. And, in another humorous twist of fate, the San Francisco Stock Exchange Luncheon Club asked Rivera to paint a mural for them. There could hardly be an organization more opposed to the ideals of communism than a capitalist stock exchange. Rivera told an American reporter that he was going to bring revolutionary art to America.

The Mexico City house in which Frida and Diego lived after they were married.

A Move Northward

Frida Kahlo was also anxious to see the
United States. In 1930, the couple moved
to California.

In San Francisco, Frida painted a wedding picture of herself and Diego. It shows
him holding a palette and paint brushes,
standing sturdy and strong in his dark suit
and large brown shoes. She is wearing a
green dress with a bright orange-red shawl.
Her head is tilted slightly toward him, as if
to show how much she cares about him.
The painting shows the contrast between
them. He was over 6 feet tall and weighed
300 pounds. She was 5 feet 3 inches and
weighed less than 100 pounds. Unlike her
other self-portraits, in which her gaze is
totally without expression, in this picture
she looks content. Floating above their
heads is a pink ribbon, called a *banderole*,
carried in the beak of a dove in flight, with
its wings apart. The ribbon is inscribed
with these words:

> Here you see us, me, Frida Kahlo,
> with my beloved husband Diego Rivera.
> I painted these portraits in the beau-
> tiful city of San Francisco, California,
> for our friend Mr. Albert Bender,
> and it was in the month of April of
> the year 1931.

Chapter 6

In the United States

Frida was a sensation on the streets of San Francisco. She swept up and down the hilly city in the vivid native Mexican skirts and blouses of the Tehuana women. She also wore bold bright jewelry, and her long black hair was often braided with colorful ribbons and flowers.

Frida in 1939.

The impression she made on the public was important to her. She dressed just as an artist composes a picture, making sure the completed image was exactly what she wanted it to be. Heads turned when she walked by. She intended them to.

Rivera liked the way Frida dressed. He said, "The classic Mexican dress has been created by people for people. The Mexican women who do not wear it do not belong to the people, but are mentally and emotionally dependent on a foreign class to which they wish to belong, [which is] the great American and French bureaucracy."

(Opposite page)
Frida's portrait of Luther Burbank, the American scientist who was famous for breeding new varieties of fruits and vegetables.

45

The way Frida dressed started a popular fashion that spread through the United States and Europe. Ironically, the women who dressed like she did, in imitation of the poor natives of Mexico, were probably among the wealthiest in the world. They were mostly members of the American and French classes that Diego Rivera scorned.

New Friends

With Rivera totally absorbed in his work and in being a celebrity, Frida was often left on her own. She explored the city and its museums and met new people. Among her new friends was a surgeon, Dr. Leo Eloesser, to whom she became devoted. She painted his portrait and gave it to him as a gift. She also painted Luther Burbank, who was famous for breeding hybrid fruits and vegetables—new plants he developed by mixing the seeds of different kinds of plants together. In a portrait of him, Frida shows Burbank as a man growing from a tree that has grown out of a human skeleton. The image of Burbank himself as a hybrid makes the picture funny. The idea that life and death are so closely linked is more serious. This painting is the first one in which Frida painted with a fantastic, surrealistic vision.

❖

The way Frida dressed started a popular fashion that spread through the United States and Europe.

On the Move

Living in San Francisco did not please Frida, however. She wrote an old friend at home, "I don't particularly like the gringo [white] people. They are boring and they all have faces like unbaked rolls. . . ."

After returning back home in June 1931, Frida and Diego started to build a house of their own. However, they stayed in Mexico for just a short time. Rivera was asked to exhibit his works at the Museum of Modern Art (MOMA), and the couple set sail for New York City that November.

As the guests of honor at many social gatherings, they met the richest and most famous Americans. Frida wrote Dr. Eloesser soon after they arrived: "Diego naturally is already at work and the city has interested him greatly and me likewise, but I, as always, never do anything except look and get bored. . . ." In a later letter she told the doctor, "High society here turns me off and I feel a bit of rage against all these rich guys here, since I have seen thousands of people in the most terrible misery. . . ."

Despite her complaints, Frida had a dazzling time going out to lunch and to the movies with friends. Then Diego was asked to paint murals in Detroit, the center of the thriving automobile industry.

❖

While in Detroit, Frida and Diego had an encounter with prejudice.

To Rivera and many other artists and intellectuals of that era, the machinery of mass production held the promise of jobs and a better life for the working class. Factories and machines themselves were admired as works of beauty. Tall brick smokestacks, glistening steel turbines, precisely engineered pistons, and perfectly balanced wheels became the subjects for painters and photographers.

While in Detroit, Frida and Diego had an encounter with prejudice. Their hotel discriminated against Jews. Rivera shouted at the management that both he and his wife were part Jewish as they angrily prepared to leave. When the hotel keeper offered to lower the rent if they would remain, they refused. Finally, the hotel agreed to change its anti-Semitic (against Jews) policy, and the couple agreed to stay.

Frida was still as outspoken as she had been in school. She lectured anyone who annoyed her, from the elevator operator to the most powerful men in the United States. Henry Ford, the tycoon responsible for mass production in the automobile industry, was a well-known anti-Semite. Rivera enjoyed telling about how Frida once turned to Ford at a dinner party and loudly asked, "Mr. Ford, are you Jewish?"

Another Tragedy

While they were living in Detroit, Frida discovered that she was pregnant. She knew that pregnancy was risky for her because of her injuries. At first she planned to have an abortion. A doctor in Detroit persuaded her that she could carry a baby successfully, and she decided to try. With her independent spirit, she also insisted on learning to drive, although the doctor had advised her to stay at home and rest.

When she was three and a half months pregnant, Frida suffered unbearable pain and bleeding. Rushed to the hospital by ambulance in the early hours of the morning of July 4, 1932, she had a miscarriage. It was the third major physical tragedy of her life. She spent 13 days in the hospital and fell into a terrible depression.

With her incredible strength of character, Frida pulled herself out of this depression and began to paint. Her work became extraordinarily powerful and unusual. She now began to paint from the depth of her experience, expressing ideas with images that were hers alone.

In one new painting, called *Henry Ford Hospital*, Frida is lying naked on a hospital bed in the picture. Although her face is typically without expression, a large tear runs down her cheek. On the far horizon is the industrial skyline. The sky looks neither forbidding nor warm. The ground is simply brown and empty. Along the frame of the bed, Frida has written the name of the hospital in which she had her miscarriage—Henry Ford Hospital Detroit. The sheet below her is spattered with blood. In her hand she holds blood-red ribbons. Six strange objects float at the ends of the ribbons. Each object symbolizes something about the awful loss that she experienced. The unborn baby, a pink shape representing her own body, and the bones of her pelvis are easily interpreted. The other three objects are less obvious. A snail may represent the slow progress of the miscarriage and the slow deterioration of her body. The odd piece of machinery on the floor may have something to do with the crushing pain she felt. It may also express the idea of an industrial city. In addition, Rivera had brought her a purple orchid at the hospital. That object is also included in the painting.

Henry Ford Hospital, and another painting called *My Birth,* launched a new phase in Frida Kahlo's painting. She began to paint *My Birth* during another sad time.

Her mother had become seriously ill. In

1932, two months after Frida's miscarriage, and one month before her mother died, Frida returned home to Mexico.

My Birth has many interpretations. The woman giving birth could be Frida's mother, whose death is shown by the sheet over her head. But the image also brings to mind the baby that Frida lost. In this case, it would be Frida's head that is covered as a way of showing her grief.

Frida began painting on small pieces of tin. She had adapted a Mexican religious tradition of offering pictures by way of thanks. These *retablos* show a disaster, such as illness or accidents, which has been survived. Usually a portrait of a particular saint or of the Virgin or Christ is part of the painting.

Frida adapted the tin *retablos* from the popular folk art of Mexican peasants. *Retablos* are usually no larger than a book. Both their size and their subject matter make them a very personal kind of art.

Frida's art was extremely personal. It was also clearly female. A man could not have conceived, or even explored, the themes of her paintings. From the deep well of her own personal tragedies, Frida Kahlo was discovering her unique artistic hand. It was both singular and universal.

Chapter 7

Her Own Reality

Perhaps Frida Kahlo painted to stay sane. Maybe painting was her personal painkiller. Certainly painting helped her to endure great tragedy.

A detail from *Self-Portrait with Monkey.*

After Diego had finished his work in Detroit, he was asked to paint a mural on the RCA building in New York City's Rockefeller Center. Support for the project came from industrialist John D. Rockefeller. His son, Nelson, was put in charge of arrangements for the mural. Nelson Rockefeller defined the theme of the painting as "Men at the Crossroads looking with Hope and High Vision to the Choosing of a New and Better Future."

Much controversy over Diego's mural was provoked by a headline in the *New York World-Telegram.* It read, "Rivera Paints Scenes of Communist Activity and John D. Jr. Foots Bill." Diego's mural became a heated

(Opposite page) **Frida painted *Self-Portrait with Monkey* in 1940.**

Rivera at work on his giant mural in Rockefeller Center in 1933. The mural became the center of a great scandal and was never completed.

political issue. People argued about it on the streets outside the RCA building. Then Diego began to paint a portrait of the Russian Communist leader Lenin on one of the figures in the mural. Nelson Rockefeller asked Diego to substitute another face for that of Lenin, but Diego refused. He was ordered to stop working. The Rockefellers paid him off and fired him. There were protest meetings and a public outcry for and against the mural. Many intellectuals of the day supported Diego. However, the Rockefellers held their ground, and the entire painting, which was two-thirds finished, was soon destroyed.

A Troubled Marriage

Diego's anger and disappointment took its toll on the marriage. He also began seeing another woman. At the same time, Frida was once again in physical pain. Her right foot was giving her trouble and she had to stay off of it. Adding to her misery was the awful homesickness she felt for Mexico. In a painting called *My Dress Hangs There,* she expressed her longing to be back home. The dress hangs above a scene representing the United States, but she is not in it.

Diego, in contrast, had little interest in going back to Mexico. The couple argued bitterly about leaving. Finally, they went home in December 1933. Diego complained that Frida had pressured him to return. They moved into their new home, which was in fact two houses. His house was painted pink and hers was blue. His was also the larger of the two.

Then Diego did something very cruel and painful to Frida. He had a love affair with Frida's youngest sister, Cristina. Part of Frida's reaction was physical. She cut off her beautiful, long black hair and stopped wearing the colorful Tehuana dresses that had been her trademark.

Frida expressed her feelings in a gory painting called *A Few Small Nips.* It pictures a woman stabbed to death by her boyfriend and is based on an actual murder. The title came from the words of the murderer. He said, as if innocent, that he had only given her "a few small nips." Those words appear on the banner above the bed. As in the picture she painted of her marriage to Diego, birds hold the ends of the banner. One bird is a dove. The other looks like the blackbird Diego compared to Frida's eyebrows. It is the shape Frida used to symbolize herself.

Adding to Frida's misery was the awful homesickness she felt for Mexico.

Frida and Diego separated several times. She also had love affairs. One affair was with Russian revolutionary leader, Leon Trotsky. Unconventional and defiant, Frida had affairs with women as well as men.

As her body seemed to slowly self-destruct, Frida was in and out of the hospital. Her marriage was sometimes good and sometimes bad. No matter how unfaithful he was to her as his wife, however, Diego always supported Frida as a painter.

Frida was also becoming recognized by the rest of the world as an artist in her own right. In 1939, a gallery in New York showed 25 of her paintings with great success.

André Breton, the French leader of the Surrealist style of art claimed her as part of the movement. Frida insisted she was not to be labeled Surrealist. "I never painted dreams," she once said. "I painted my own reality." She went to Paris where her work was included in a Surrealist show.

When she returned home, Diego asked for a divorce. That was when she began to paint *The Two Fridas*. As tormented as their marriage was, Frida and Diego could not stand to be apart. They remarried in 1940. However, Frida lived separately, in her parent's house in Coyoacán, when her father moved to an apartment nearby.

Frida and Diego were remarried in San Francisco, California, in 1940.

An Important Painting

Self-portrait with Monkeys was painted in 1943. In the background are thick, yellow-green leaves that could be growing in a jungle. A flame-orange, blue, and purple bird of paradise flower rises above Frida's shoulder. The plant, flower, and the leaves are larger than life. They surround her, almost shoving her forward.

Frida kept monkeys as pets and often included them in her self-portraits. Four small monkeys encircle her in this work. Like the dense leaves and flower, they crowd her. One monkey has wound its tail around her arm. The other has its arm around her neck. Their long, thin fingers touch her white Tehuana blouse.

These monkeys are cute, yet there is something troubling about them. They may seem to be human, but they are not. Monkeys are unclean animals. They have no moral code and no shame. You cannot predict what they will do next.

How much did Frida think about the symbolism of monkeys? That is information she did not leave behind. But it is to the credit of her paintings that they have many layers of ideas. They are as simple or as complicated as the knowledge and imagination of the person looking at them.

❖

"I never painted dreams," Frida said, "I painted my own reality."

Surrounding herself with her monkeys was partly simple fun for Frida. Some people believe they were substitutes for children. Parrots, deer, dogs, even an eagle were among her other pets. And she had a doll collection. In the painting *My Doll and Me*, the doll most certainly represents the baby Frida wished she could have.

In *Self-Portrait with Monkeys*, Frida seems to be trapped. She could be daring us to set her free. She could as easily be defying us to try. Truly, it is difficult to know whether the monkeys are guardians who protect her or demons who possess her. Perhaps they are both.

In this, as in most of her self-portraits, Kahlo sits very stiffly, as though everything would come crashing down if she moved. Within 10 years after she painted *Self-Portrait with Monkeys*, everything did fall apart.

By the early 1950s, Frida's body finally gave out. She spent an entire year in the hospital. Her leg had to be amputated (cut off). Difficult as it was, she continued to paint. In 1953, she was recognized with a show of her works in her own country. An ambulance took her to the opening celebration, where she enjoyed the party lying on a stretcher. The following year she died.

(Opposite page)
Frida's *Self-Portrait as a Tehuana*, painted in 1943, shows the strong ties she maintained with her cultural past.

Diego Rivera, the man who loved and tormented her, was deeply saddened. He said that only at her death did he realize how much Frida's love had meant to him. Yet he always knew that her art was great. Where his paintings were loud public and political statements, hers were small, quiet, personal cries. He had said that she was a better painter than he. Perhaps she was.

It was another 30 years after her death before the significance of her work finally began to make a deep impression on the world. Only today is Frida Kahlo truly recognized as one of the most imaginative, original, and heroic painters in the history of art.

Glossary

Explaining New Words

casa The Spanish word for house.

communism A political and social system in which there is little private ownership of property or business. The state controls means of production and owns major industries. A Communist is someone who believes in communism.

contemporary Events that take place during the same period. People who are alive at the same time.

epilepsy A disease that causes victims to lose control of their bodies.

fiesta A celebration or festival.

folklore Stories and beliefs that people tell over many years. Usually folklore is spoken rather than written down.

image A picture of a person or a thing.

Mesoamerican Referring to the people and lands of Central America.

miscarriage When something does not happen as it is supposed to. A term used when a pregnancy ends too early and the baby cannot be saved.

movement A group of people who believe in the same ideas and try to make those ideas known to others form a *movement.* Examples are the Communist movement and the Surrealist movement.

mural A picture or decoration painted directly onto a wall.

polio A disease of the nervous system that paralyzes its victims.

subconscious Ideas and images in a person's mind that she or he may not realize are there at the time they occur. Dreams, for example, occur in the subconscious mind.

Surrealism A literary and artistic movement in which artists are said express the subconscious mind.

Tehuana Native Mexican tribe around which much folklore is based.

theme The idea behind a story.

unconventional Someone or something who is not like most people or things.

For Further Reading

Cardona, Rudolfo, and James Cockcroft, eds. *Diego Rivera*. Broomall, Pennsylvania: Chelsea House, 1992.

Cardona, Rudolfo and James Cockcroft, eds. *Pancho Villa*. Broomall, Pennsylvania: Chelsea House, 1992.

Davis, Hawke. *Mexico City*. Austin, Texas: Raintree Steck-Vaughn, 1990.

Drucker, Malka. *Frida Kahlo*. New York: Bantam, 1991.

Odijk, Pamela. *The Aztecs*. Westwood, New Jersey: Silver Burdett Press, 1992.

Odijk, Pamela. *The Mayas*. Westwood, New Jersey: Silver Burdett Press, 1992.

Index

Photo Credits:
Cover: International Museum of Photography at George Eastman House; pp. 4, 5, 21, 32, 39, 44, 52, 53, 59: Courtesy Frida Kahlo Museum, Mexico; pp. 10, 29: © Grace How; pp. 12, 14, 15: © Gina Furszyfer; pp. 20, 22, 38, 41, 42, 45, 54, 56: AP/Wide World Photos; pp. 26 (top and bottom), 27 (top left): Art Resource; p. 27 (bottom right): Giraudon/Art Resource; p. 28: Lauros-Giraudon.

Photo research by Grace How.